P9-EDS-199

# My Little Book of
# Dogs and Puppies

by Nicola Jane Swinney

Sandy Creek
NEW YORK

**Sandy Creek**
NEW YORK

An Imprint of Sterling Publishing Co., Inc.
1166 Avenue of the Americas
New York, NY 10036

SANDY CREEK and the distinctive Sandy Creek logo
are registered trademarks of Barnes & Noble, Inc.

Text © 2016 by QEB Publishing, Inc.
Illustrations © 2016 by QEB Publishing, Inc.

All rights reserved. No part of this publication may be
reproduced, stored in a retrieval system or transmitted
in any form or by any means (including electronic,
mechanical, photocopying, recording, or otherwise)
without prior written permission from the publisher.

ISBN 978-1-4351-6414-7

Manufactured in Guangdong, China
Lot #:
2  4  6  8  10  9  7  5  3  1
06/16

www.sterlingpublishing.com

Words in **bold**
are explained
in the glossary
on page 60.

# Contents

# Introduction

Dogs make wonderful pets—they can be loving and fun friends. They are separated into **breeds**. Dogs of a particular breed look similar and have a special character.

⌄ **Some dogs are bred for their looks. Others are bred to do a particular job.**

<< Herding dogs, such as this sheepdog, are used to round up animals.

The different breeds are divided into groups. The groups include **terriers**, herding dogs, **working dogs**, and hounds (or hunting dogs).

^ Terriers were bred to chase small animals from their burrows.

# Afghan Hound

The Afghan comes from the deserts and mountains of Afghanistan. It is one of the oldest breeds of dog.

« These dogs can be shy, sensitive, and stubborn.

Like all **sighthounds**, the Afghan was bred to find prey using its eyes rather than its nose.

⌄ Afghans can run very fast. They love to chase.

⌃ The Afghan's long, silky coat needs to be brushed every day.

# Airedale

This popular breed comes from Yorkshire in England. It is named for the River Aire.

This sturdy dog is the largest terrier. It is known as the "king of terriers." It loves to romp around and enjoys going for a swim.

⌃ **The Airedale is clever and easy to train.**

⌃ This dog is
friendly and loves
to play games.

⌃ The Airedale
was bred to catch
otters and rats.

# Beagle

The beagle is a **scent hound**. It uses its nose to **track** prey. It has a better sense of smell than almost any other dog.

Beagles were bred to hunt rabbits and hares. These dogs like to hunt together in **packs**.

« This smart dog makes a very good family pet.

≪ The beagle is lively and always ready for action.

⋀ Beagles howl when they pick up the scents of their prey.

# Bernese Mountain Dog

This breed dates back 2,000 years. It was used in Switzerland for herding sheep and cattle, and for pulling small carts.

>> These dogs are kind, brave, friendly, and obedient.

>> Bernese mountain dogs remain puppy-like for several years.

⌄ Young Bernese, or "Berners," are full of energy.

The Bernese has a thick coat to keep it warm in the mountains. It has black, **tan**, and white markings.

# Border Collie

The border collie is a herding dog. It can round up lots of sheep and move, or **herd**, them where it wants them to go.

⌃ The border collie is happiest when it is herding!

The dog watches and listens for signals from the shepherd. Then it moves around the sheep very quickly to keep them together.

« Border collies can have blue or brown eyes, or one of each color!

⌃ Border collies are also called sheepdogs.

# Boxer

The boxer is energetic and fun-loving. It loves to play with its owner. It also makes a good **guard dog**.

⌄ **This big, strong dog needs lots of exercise.**

⌃ **The boxer has a short, square muzzle.**

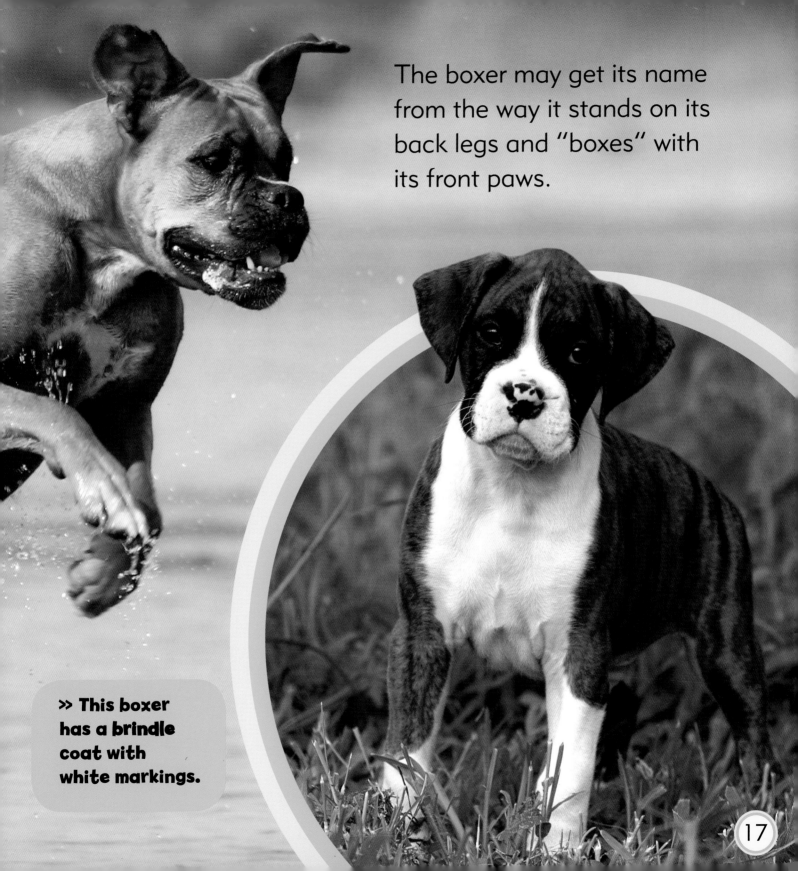

The boxer may get its name from the way it stands on its back legs and "boxes" with its front paws.

>> This boxer has a **brindle** coat with white markings.

# Chihuahua

This perky little dog is the smallest breed of dog in the world. These dogs are so small that some people carry them around in their handbags!

**⌃ These dogs often shiver when they are cold, excited, or frightened.**

**« Chihuahuas can have short or long hair.**

Chihuahuas come from Mexico, which is a hot country. They don't like to get cold or wet!

⌃ **The Chihuahua loves to follow its owner everywhere.**

# Cocker Spaniel

The cocker spaniel is related to the English cocker spaniel. It is a gentle, loving dog with a long, silky coat.

⌄ **This dog's coat tangles easily and needs to be brushed every day.**

« **The cocker spaniel has lots of energy and enjoys agility jumps.**

The cocker spaniel is the smallest breed of **gun dog**. It was bred by hunters to carry birds in its mouth.

˄ The cocker spaniel loves to bring back, or **retrieve**, a ball.

# Dachshund

The popular nickname for the Dachshund is "wiener dog," because of its long body.

⌄ **There are three types—long-haired (left), wirehaired (center), and short-haired (right).**

It was bred this shape so it could hunt for badgers in their tunnels.

≪ These dogs are active and fun-loving. They may bark loudly at strangers.

⌃ Dachshunds may be small, but they are brave and bold.

# Dalmatian

This spotted dog can run for miles.
Long ago, in England, dalmatians used
to run beside horse-drawn carriages and
protect the passengers from robbers.

« Dalmatians
need firm
training when
they are young.

It is a friendly breed and loves to be with people. It needs lots of exercise. A dalmatian would be a good pet for someone who likes to hike long distances with a dog.

⌃ **Puppies are born white. Spots appear after about three weeks.**

⌃ **These dogs never seem to get tired.**

# Golden Retriever

⌄ The "smily" mouth is typical of a golden retriever.

This friendly dog makes a wonderful family pet. It is a smart dog and loves people.

« These dogs hold things gently in their mouths.

Golden retrievers are known as "goldens" for short. They stay puppy-like and playful for many years.

>> This breed is always happy to play, especially in water.

27

# Great Dane

This breed of dog is huge! It's often called a gentle giant. It was originally bred to be big, strong, and brave so that it could hunt wild boar.

« **Male Great Danes usually grow 30 to 33 inches tall.**

The world's tallest Great Dane measured 44 inches from paw to shoulder—that's the size of an average donkey! These dogs are calm and loving, and make great pets.

« At birth, a Great Dane puppy weighs one or two pounds. By six months old, it can weigh 100 pounds!

⌃ The color of this Great Dane is known as blue.

# Husky

This dog has amazing eyes! They are as blue as the ice in Siberia and Alaska, where the dog comes from.

⌃ **Huskies can pull sleds for miles across ice. They work in teams.**

« **Huskies have lots of energy. They need a lot of exercise each day.**

Huskies like to live with people and other dogs. They like to feel they are part of a group, or pack.

>> This dog's extra-thick coat keeps it warm in very cold weather.

# Irish Wolfhound

This is the tallest of all dog breeds. It was originally bred in Ireland to hunt wolves and Irish elk (an **extinct** type of deer).

>> Male wolfhounds can measure up to 35 inches from paw to shoulder.

When the last wolf in Ireland was killed in about 1800, the wolfhound almost died out. Luckily it was saved, and today it is a popular pet.

≪ This dog loves its family. It is calm and dignified.

⋀ Wolfhounds never curl up! They prefer to stretch out.

# Jack Russell

This bouncy, tough little dog is a terrier. It has a big personality, lots of energy, and it likes to be kept busy.

« Jack Russells are mainly white, with black and tan markings.

« These are smart and fearless dogs.

The Jack Russell was bred to chase red foxes out of their burrows. It loves to play games of chase or catch.

« Jack Russells enjoy a good run. They often bark to get attention.

# Labrador

The Labrador was originally bred by fishermen to haul fishing nets and carry ropes. Today, working Labradors are used by hunters to bring back, or retrieve, birds.

« This Labrador puppy has a chocolate-colored coat.

Labradors make wonderful pets. They can also be trained to work as **assistance dogs** for handicapped people.

∧ Labradors are friendly, loving, and loyal. They have very sweet natures.

# Old English Sheepdog

This big, cuddly-looking dog needs plenty of exercise. It has a long, shaggy coat that needs lots of brushing.

« This dog was bred to help farmers drive sheep and cattle to market.

It has a deep, booming bark, and likes to protect its family. This makes it a good guard dog.

≪ This dog drools a lot. The drool can turn its coat yellow.

⌃ The puppies learn quickly and like to be kept busy.

# Pekingese

Although it is small, this dog is said to have the heart of a lion. For hundreds of years they were kept by the emperors of China.

« The Pekingese has a long mane like a lion, and is very brave.

Chinese emperors used to carry their Pekingese dogs in the sleeve cuffs of their long robes.

⌄ Pekingese, or Pekes, have flat noses. This makes them snore loudly.

« These dogs are playful, but also stubborn and difficult to train.

# Pinscher

Pinscher is the German word for "terrier." There are various pinscher breeds, including the German pinscher.

⌃ A German pinscher puppy needs to be trained early, otherwise it may try to control its owner.

The German pinscher is much bigger than most terriers. It is a sturdy and elegant dog, with a smooth, glossy coat.

« This obedient dog makes an excellent guard dog.

⌃ A devoted family dog, it loves to play— even as an adult.

# Pug

Long ago, pugs were owned only by China's royal family. Now they are popular all over the world.

^ The pug has large, round eyes and a flat nose.

Some people call pugs "clowns," because they love to be the centers of attention.

⌄ **Pugs shed a lot of hair from their coats.**

⌃ **Pugs are smart but stubborn. They like to do things their own way.**

# Rottweiler

The Rottweiler, or Rottie, looks fierce but is easy to train. Rotties are often used as guard dogs, **guide dogs** for blind people, or **police dogs**.

⌄ **This strong dog was bred to pull butchers' carts to market.**

⌃ **Rotties should be given an hour of exercise every day.**

In the past, soldiers used these brave dogs to carry messages during wartime. They also trained them to collect wounded soldiers from battlefields.

⌄ **Rottie puppies need to meet other dogs. This helps them to be friendly when they are older.**

# Schnauzer

The Schnauzer comes from Germany. It was bred to herd cattle and to guard farmhouses and stables.

« This dog has a wiry coat that comes in "salt and pepper" shades.

Schnauzers were also used to pull small farm carts and catch rats. They make good all-around farm dogs.

<< The Schnauzer learns quickly and makes a great pet.

ʌ This dog will give a deep bark if it hears strange noises.

# Shih Tzu

This dog is a bundle of fluff! The shih tzu has a long, flowing coat and a curved tail. Left to grow, its coat would reach the ground.

« Some people prefer to clip their shih tzu's coat.

» This dog is no good at hunting, guarding, or herding. It just wants to be your friend.

It is a bouncy, friendly dog, and makes a loyal and loving pet. Its small size makes it a good choice of dog for people who live in apartments.

⌃ **The shih tzu's hair needs to be brushed every day.**

# Springer Spaniel

Springer spaniels are gentle and loving dogs. They are also bouncy and full of energy.

Springers were bred as hunting dogs. They were trained to startle, or "spring," birds on the ground to make them fly up into the air.

<< This springer has been groomed for a dog show.

≪ Springers love water. They will leap in whenever they get the chance.

⌄ Springers are alert and eager to please.

# Standard Poodle

There are three sizes of poodle. The "standard" is the biggest. Next is the "miniature." The smallest is the "toy."

>> Standard poodles are cheerful and easy to train.

<< A standard poodle's coat is curly and does not shed hairs.

Poodles are known for their fancy haircuts. Sometimes they are clipped so that they have pom-poms on their feet and tail tips.

⌃ These dogs respond well to owners who are calm but firm.

55

# Vizsla

The vizsla comes from Hungary, where it was used as a gun dog for hundreds of years. It is known as a "velcro dog," because it likes to stick close to its owner.

« This dog makes a lively and loving pet.

∨ **The vizsla is happiest when it has a job to do!**

This smart dog is easy to train. It has a good sense of smell and can be used as a **search-and-rescue dog**.

≫ **Vizslas can either be wirehaired, like this one, or have a smooth coat.**

# Yorkshire Terrier

Don't be fooled by its size! The Yorkshire terrier, or Yorkie, has a big personality.

˅ **There are usually between one and four puppies in a Yorkie litter.**

Yorkies like to protect their owners. They often bark at visitors or sudden noises.

<< Yorkies love to chase squirrels, and sometimes other dogs!

^ The Yorkie has a long, silky coat of fine hair.

# Glossary

**agility** A sport in which dogs go over an obstacle course in a timed race.

**assistance dogs** These dogs are specially trained to help people with disabilities.

**blue** A darkish gray coat.

**breed** Dogs of a particular breed, or type, that look similar.

**brindle** A black and brown striped coat.

**chocolate** A dark brown coat.

**dog show** An event where dogs are shown off in a ring and are judged for their looks or skills.

**drool** A clear, thick liquid that dribbles from a dog's mouth.

**extinct** No longer existing.

**guard dog** A dog trained to protect a place.

**guide dogs** Dogs that have been trained to help blind people walk safely.

**gun dogs** Dogs trained to bring back birds shot by hunters.

**herd** To move animals where you want them to go.

**litter** The puppies born to a dog at a single time.

**muzzle** The nose and jaws.

**obedient** Happy to do what it is being told to do.

**pack** A group of dogs that live and sometimes work together.

**police dogs** Dogs that have been trained to help police find or guard things.

**retrieve** To find something and bring it back.

**scent hound** A dog that tracks by following a scent.

**search-and-rescue dog** A dog that helps find missing people after a disaster, such as an earthquake.

**sighthounds** Dogs that see and then chase an animal, rather than following a scent.

**tan** Light brown.

**terriers** Dogs bred to hunt animals that live in burrows.

**track** To follow the traces an animal has left behind, such as its scent.

**working dogs** Dogs bred to do jobs such as guarding or pulling sleds.

# Index

# Picture credits

(t=top, b=bottom, l=left, r=right, c=center, fc=front cover, bc=back cover)

**Alamy**
50l © David J. Green - animals / Alamy Stock Photo.

**Bob & Pam Langrish KA9 Photo**
13r ©Bob & Pam Langrish_KA9 Photo

**FLPA**
1 /Imagebroker/FLPA, 2 Chris Brignell/FLPA, 3 ImageBroker/Imagebroker/FLPA, 6/7 /Imagebroker/FLPA, 7r Ramona Richter/Tierfotoagentur/FLPA, 8/9 Ramona Richter/Tierfotoagentur/FLPA, 9r Chris Brignell/FLPA, 10l Ramona Richter/Tierfotoagentur/FLPA, 12r ImageBroker/Imagebroker/FLPA, 12/13 Bernd Brinkmann/Imagebroker/FLPA, 14/15 Melanie Bayer/Tierfotoagentur/FLPA, 15r Bernd Brinkmann/Imagebroker/FLPA, 16l /Imagebroker/FLPA, 16/17 Dana Geithner/Tierfotoagentur/FLPA, 18tr /Imagebroker/FLPA, 19 Jeanette Hutfluss/Tierfotoagentur/FLPA, 22l Gerard Lacz/FLPA, 22/23 Jeanette Hutfluss/Tierfotoagentur/FLPA, 23r Ramona Richter/Tierfotoagentur/FLPA, 24l Chris Brignell/FLPA, 24/25 Ramona Richter/Tierfotoagentur/FLPA, 25r Marion Fichter/Imagebroker/FLPA, 26r ImageBroker/Imagebroker/FLPA, 27 David Hosking/FLPA, 28l Ramona Richter/Tierfotoagentur/FLPA, 28/29 Chris Brignell/FLPA, 29r /Imagebroker/FLPA, 30/31 Imagebroker, Kerstin Langenberger/Imagebroker/FLPA, 31r Mareike Wegner/Tierfotoagentur/FLPA, 33l /Imagebroker/FLPA, 33r Marion Fichter/Imagebroker/FLPA, 34l /Imagebroker/FLPA, 34/35 Nina Schmaus/Tierfotoagentur/FLPA, 36l Kerstin Luhrs/Tierfotoagentur/FLPA, 36/37 Mitsuaki Iwago/Minden Pictures/FLPA, 38/39 Mark Raycroft/Minden Pictures/FLPA, 39r Erica Olsen/FLPA, 40l David Dalton/FLPA, 40/41 Melanie Bayer/Tierfotoagentur/FLPA, 41r Melanie Bayer/Tierfotoagentur/FLPA, 42l Jeanette Hutfluss/Tierfotoagentur/FLPA, 42/43 Jeanette Hutfluss/Tierfotoagentur/FLPA, 43r Mark Raycroft/Minden Pictures/FLPA, 44/45 PICANI/Imagebroker/FLPA, 45r Nicole Jeanette Noack/Tierfotoagentur/FLPA, 46l Daniela Jakob/Tierfotoagentur/FLPA, 47r Jeanette Hutfluss/Tierfotoagentur/FLPA, 48l Mark Raycroft/Minden Pictures/FLPA, 48/49 PICANI/Imagebroker/FLPA, 49r Ramona Richter/Tierfotoagentur/FLPA, 51r Gerard Lacz/FLPA, 52/53 Erica Olsen/FLPA, 53r Jeanette Hutfluss/Tierfotoagentur/FLPA, 54/55 Michaela Kuhn/Tierfotoagentur/FLPA, 56l Angela Hampton/FLPA, 56/57 Jeanette Hutfluss/Tierfotoagentur/FLPA, 57r Angela Hampton/FLPA, 64 John Eveson/FLPA.

**Getty Images**
Mark Raycroft: 8l, 11r, 17r, 18bl, 20/21, 30l, 35r, 38l, 44l, 46/47, 52l, 55r, 59r.

**Shutterstock**
4/5 cynoclub, 5tl Katrina Leigh, 5br Husakou, 6l otsphoto, 10/11 Lunja, 14l Katrina Leigh, 20l cynoclub, 21r Daz Stock, 26l rokopix , 32 Jana Oudova, 50/51 Eric Isselee, 54l JLSnader, 58l Pelevina Ksinia, 58/59 Daz Stock.